A TRUCKER'S DREAM

BY

SHARON JANK

ISBN: 979-8-8693-7839-2

Dedication

For my dad, Charlie Tuna.

Contents

Introduction

Buddy is a small town trucker in Tennessee, working for a big grocery store. He has worked hard to provide for a better life for his family. His dream is to start his own trucking business. Then, tragedy happens, the unimaginable but real-to-life turn of events. This book is fictional, but the contents are genuine to our everyday lives. Occasionally, we take for granted how we get food and supplies to our families and the comforts of living in America. I also hope this book makes you think about free enterprise and capitalism in our country. Last but not least, we must respect our law enforcement, they are sometimes working on a case for years for the justice of the victims.

Chapter 1
The Dream

It is Christmas Eve; Buddy is in his bedroom with his three-year-old daughter. The house is decorated. There's a Christmas tree. There are presents opened on the floor. The house looks as if a party took place in it. Yet, the surroundings are quiet and calm. There are leftover plates in the kitchen that are uncleaned. The cake is left on a plate, too.

Buddy is lying on his bed with his daughter, who's holding a cute little teddy bear. This is when his phone rings, "Hey, What's up?" Buddy says. "Hey, can you take a load?" the man asks on the phone. "Well, it's Christmas Eve, and I don't have a babysitter," answers Buddy.

Just as Buddy is talking on the phone, he looks at the mantel in front of him, which has pictures of him and his wife, Meredith. He starts having flashbacks of his old memories. He recalls the time when they purchased their new home. Buddy feels lost when he stares at the picture of

Meredith looking pregnant and putting Christmas angels on a Christmas tree.

"Buddy, are you up for this haul or not?" The man on the phone asks. Buddy gets back to his senses. He takes a long breath before answering. "Where, and how much?" Says Buddy with a bizarre look on his face. He instantly goes back to his memories and remembers how he used to work for a grocery store.

He remembers how it was his wife and his dream to have their own business and trucks. He recalls walking into the trucker diner with a neat, clean uniform. Everyone greets him when he enters, and a waitress asks him, "Any news yet, Buddy?" "No, waiting on everything this Christmas. The loan for the truck and our baby girl." Says Buddy to the waitress. In his memory lane, he goes home on Christmas Eve. Meredith is in the house, running out of the door excitedly. "We got the loan; we got the loan, baby!" Says

Meredith to Buddy. He gets happy, hugs, lifts, and spins her around.

Both of them are happy. They are inside the house. It's time for dinner, and Meredith has finished decorating the Christmas tree. So many beautiful toys are placed under the tree, and a teddy bear is wrapped in a pink ribbon. Everything is going well. As soon as Meredith puts an angel on the tree, she feels a bit odd and touches her belly. She looks down between her legs and turns back slowly to Buddy, "Babe, I think I'm in labor," Meredith says with a shaking and nervous voice. Buddy gets excited, but he's nervous too. Buddy recalls grabbing the baby bag and Meredith's stuff and getting inside the car with her. They are on the way to the hospital. Meredith is having labor pains. He calls his family with excitement.

As soon as they reach the hospital, the staff and doctors start the procedure. Meredith is in the labor room with Buddy. His family has arrived. Everyone's excited and happy. The doctor hands a beautiful, healthy baby girl to her parents. Buddy looks at his daughter with excitement. This is when the doctors feel there is something wrong with Meredith. "We cannot stop the bleeding, Buddy. You have to leave the room for a while," says the doctor to Buddy. "What happened to my wife?" Buddy asks the doctor immediately. "We have to attend to Meredith. Give us some time," the doctor responds. Buddy leaves the room and gives them the space to work.

While Buddy walks outside the operation room, he's worried for his wife and daughter. It's almost twenty minutes, and the nurse comes out of the room. "Buddy, there's a problem with Meredith. We cannot stop the bleeding. She was taken into surgery, but there's nothing we can do at this moment. You have to come inside and talk with your wife so she may feel better," says the nurse.

Tears fall from Buddy's eyes as he walks inside to see Meredith. Everything is suddenly slowing down as

Buddy feels someone yelling on the phone. He blinks his eyes and realizes he's on a call that's offering him a job. Another blink, and he's back in the room where Meredith is lying on the hospital bed. She's pale, and her face looks exhausted. "Name her," Meredith says. Buddy is standing in the hospital room looking at Meredith when he hears someone yelling his name, "Buddy, Buddy! Do you want the job or not? Can you take the job?" Says the man on the phone. And Buddy comes back from his memory lane and stands up. "Yeah, I'll take it. I would have to bring my daughter with me." Buddy answers the guy on the phone while looking at his daughter. The call disconnects.

Buddy is still standing, feeling slightly numb when his daughter tries to have his attention. "Dada?" The three-year-old speaks. Buddy looks at his daughter and smiles, "Dada? Come here, my angel." Buddy holds his daughter in his arms while looking at the picture of Meredith.

Chapter 2
The Country Haul

Buddy decides to take the job and packs his and the baby's stuff to be on their way. He puts his daughter on a baby seat and buckles her up. He feeds her milk, so she sleeps fine all along the way. He gets into the truck and starts driving toward their destination.

Buddy is driving on a dark, tense road, the weather is foggy, and it's raining as well. No cars are on the road as it's Christmas Eve, and everyone is enjoying their family time at home while Buddy is on his way to work. His daughter is holding a teddy bear as she sleeps. He is thinking about his wife, who had passed away, and about his business; he wants to have his own trucking company and wants to own his own trucks. He is gathering the motivation to get through this trip for his daughter and his business. He is processing his thoughts and not focusing on the road. Just as he's lost in his thoughts, he fails to observe a deer on the road. He tries to slow down, but he loses control of the truck and slips down sideways, which takes his truck down the mountain. He hits many trees that also try to block his way, falling down the mountain. Suddenly, he hits a big tree that smashes the front window and breaks the glass of the side mirror as well. Buddy got a hit on his head that made his vision blurry. The truck is stuck on the edge of a big tree on the mountain, smoke is coming out of the engine, and no one notices that a truck has just slid off from the mountain.

Buddy is stuck in the truck with his daughter; she's crying badly as Buddy looks over the angel hanging in front of his truck. He says, "Don't worry, Mommy angel is watching over us. Everything's going to be alright." This is when a couple was going from the same road and observed that there were truck marks on the road, and the sideways were destroyed as if something hit it. They stopped and found Buddy's truck had slid down. The husband rushes carefully to the truck as he hears the baby crying. He goes near the truck and sees there is a baby girl and a guy who's been badly hit. He tries to open the doors, but they are stuck among the trees. Then, he tries to make his way through the broken window from Buddy's seat. He unbuckles his belt and gets him out of the truck. Then he goes inside carefully to carry his daughter. Buddy is lying on the ground, catching his last breath. He loses visions of reality and sees a glimpse of his wife giving her hand for him to hold. This is when Buddy hears his daughter cry and looks over at the man holding his daughter while taking his last breath. Buddy is gone. The man tries to see if he's still breathing, but he is no longer breathing. He's gone; his heartbeat had stopped. Instead of calling an ambulance, the man calls out to his wife to come down and help him with the baby. She comes down slowly and feels awful about the entire situation. The man grabs the baby's bag and asks his wife to go up with him. The wife is scared and terrified. She asks her husband if they should call an ambulance or inform the police, but the man asks her to sit in the car.

His wife screams while he puts the baby in the car and goes to sit in the driving seat. The wife first sits in the passenger seat, looking at her husband and thinking, what the hell is he doing? Then she sees the baby crying badly, goes out the door, and sits at the back to comfort her. And her husband takes off. Buddy is still lying down on the edge of the mountain near his truck, and no one can help him at this point.

Chapter 3

The Angel in
the Sky

It's daylight, the night has passed, and a person is going by as he notices an accident has happened. He pulls over and sees a truck down the mountain. The day sky had the feel of stillness and calmness of a moment just before a torrential downpour. He panics and calls 911, immediately informing them about the situation. The police arrive with ambulances, paramedics, helpers, and emergency workers. The road is closed, and the traffic has been re-routed. A local Sheriff comes from the area where Buddy lies dead. Buddy has passed away, and they are cutting the tree branch and pulling it away from the windshield. They bring a heavy vehicle to pull the truck back on the road. They have finally pulled the truck back, and it's in a really bad condition. The engine of the truck is destroyed, and Buddy is lying there in his cold, dead body. The Sheriff and the investigators are trying to figure out what happened; they noticed a teddy bear in the back seat, which indicates there may be a child in the car. The paramedics have declared that Buddy is dead; he is badly injured as he took a major hit on his head. They are carrying him to the hospital, where an autopsy will be performed on him to help the investigation case. The detectives and the investigators are looking at this situation in multiple scenarios. The Sheriff goes back to his office to gather more information on Buddy and where he works. The investigators are clicking pictures of Buddy's dead body, collecting evidence that could help in figuring out what happened.

There was chaos and madness, and all that they could figure out was there may be a child inside the truck, but was no longer there. The bags in the car tell that Buddy is traveling somewhere. What they don't know is where and why he was traveling on Christmas Eve, late at night. Was there a child in the truck?

Chapter 4
New Identity

Thirteen years later, Molly walks down the street outside a little town in South Dakota with her friends. It's Chris, Darren, and Molly. She's young and has long dark hair and big brown eyes. She carries a guitar, and they are coming home from school. It's Christmas; the houses are beautifully decorated. The kids are asking one another what they are doing for Christmas. This is when Molly tells them when it's her turn, "You guys know that my parents don't celebrate. We don't celebrate holidays and birthdays." Chris replied, "Oh, that's too bad. We would have you over to our house for our Christmas party?"

Molly responds, "That's alright, I'm fine. I'll practice my songs. You know I am going to be a country singer someday. So, I gotta practice, practice, and practice." They get to Molly's house, and she says, "Goodbye, you guys." She goes into her house. At the same time, her friends continue to walk down the street. Darren says, "Isn't it weird that her parents don't celebrate anything?"

Chris, "I have heard that before. It's like Jehovah's Witness or something like that. Well, see you guys," Chris ran off to her home on the street. Her mother opens the door, and she goes in. It's a well-decorated Christmas house. Chris pops out a question, "Mom, what is that religious group that doesn't celebrate any birthdays or holidays? Is that Jehovah's Witness?" "Yeah, I think it is," her mom replied. "I feel sad for Molly. She never gets to have any decorations, neither any holidays nor birthdays," Chris says. "You know, you're right. Maybe I'll bring them a plate of cookies," Chris responded, "Yeah, I think that's okay. Thanks, Mom."

Chris runs to her room. At the same time, her mother prepares a plate of cookies and goes across the street to Molly's house. Her house is a little bit down the road. There is the land between them. She walks over there and knocks on Molly's front door. Molly's mother answers, "Hi, I am Chris's mom. We just wanted to share some extra cookies. She was being careful not to say Christmas. We wanted to share them with you." Chris's mom says. While Molly's mother responds, "Oh no, that's okay. We can't accept anything. We don't celebrate these holidays." Her father also joined the conversation. "Yeah, that's right. Thank you, however. Have a great day," Molly's father shuts the door, and both parents go into the kitchen to argue.

"I told you if Molly started hanging out with people, they were going to start snooping around. I got to make a phone call," the father goes to make a phone call, and Molly is in her bedroom. However, she hears all of this. She opened the door slowly and saw her father off the phone. "Listen, we are short on money. My friend said that he could get us out of our debt. He would take good care of Molly. And you know, help her get into college and the whole bit. We got to get out of here, and we got to get out of here tonight. Molly is hearing all this, and she doesn't believe what she's hearing. She closed the door, and her parents had a hint that she may be listening to them. She runs off into her bed, puts her headphones on, and puts the guitar on her lap.

She turns on the radio and pretends that her headphones are loud and she has not heard anything. Her parents took a peek at the door, and they saw her sitting on the bed, playing her guitar. They shut the door and went back into the kitchen to plan. "You know, we got to start getting packed up; leave when it starts to get dark. Nobody notices." As soon as it gets dark, Molly grabs whatever she can get in her backpack money and takes her guitar. She heads out her bedroom door and runs to a Greyhound bus station in South Dakota.

Chapter 5
California Dreaming

Molly fled South Dakota on various Grey Hound buses. She had already prepared herself to jump onto another bus in case her parents came following her, but that wasn't very likely to happen. As she slept at night on the Grey Hound buses, she often dreamt about the memories of happiness. She dreamed of her father holding her, and sometimes she was having a birthday party. Other times, she saw herself in a dream, sitting in a vehicle and listening to country music.

When she arrived at the California Beach town, she got off the bus and started walking down the street. She reaches the seashore, walking with an empty head, gazing at a distance with an aimless mind. Some kids hanging around at the beach came over to her and asked, "Hey, how are you doing?"

"I'm good, thanks!" she replied.

The kids look at her up and down as if scanning her whole being with their eyes, wanting to inquire what was going inside her head. After a few seconds, they ask her, "Hey, do you want some marijuana?"

"Nawww! Thanks."

The wandering kids turn their back on her after realizing that she isn't interested in hanging around with them. As soon as they turn around to move away, Molly at once finds it an opportunity to ask them about a place to live. She says, "Hey, I was wondering if I could get some help here."

"Sure. What is it?" They answered.

"I am looking for a place to stay."

"Hmm. Yeah, sure, we'll help you with that. But first, how about hanging out with us for a little bit?"

Molly thought these kids would be harmless to hang out with for a while. So, she moved forward and took a look around. She saw some kids playing volleyball while others were on their skateboards. When she was done looking around, they asked her, "Hey, what's your name?"

"Name's Molly. I came here to pursue my singing career."

The bunch of kids burst out laughing, saying, "Welcome to California. There are tons of people who come here every year with the same dream. Makes no difference."

Before Molly starts feeling disappointed and losing hope, a girl named Kristin comes over and grabs her hand, pulling her back. Molly is not surprised to realize why someone pulled her that hard. At first, she tried to recognize this girl, thinking she might have known her from somewhere.

"Are you hungry?" asked Kristin.

"Hmm, yeah. I'm starving," Molly nods with full force as if she had longed for food for so long.

"I've got some health bars here. Wanna try?"

"I'd love to."

"Hey, you want to play volleyball?"

"Ah, no. I'm good. Actually, I've been traveling a long way, and I'm exhausted." Molly answered.

"Ah, well. Let's take you to my place. It's not much, but you can crash there until you find a job."

"Sure. That would be awesome. You guys are great. Thank you."

Molly picked up her bag pack, crunching on her health bar with her guitar on her back, and went with Kristin, following her lead.

"We all bunk together in small apartments around here. It is too expensive to live near the beach. But we're not too far," said Kristin.

Molly and Kristin headed out. Kristin took her to a restaurant and said, "This is where you can find a job. Dishwashing, cleaning, etc."

"I don't care. I'm just glad to be here."

"Have you run away from your home? Are your parents looking for you?"

"Nah! It's cool." I doubt anyone is looking for me.

So, Kristin and Molly make it to Kristin's apartment. Molly found out it wasn't much as to what Kristin had said. Her apartment felt like as if a cyclone had twisted it inside out. The clothes were lying and stinking up the whole room, thrown away in the corner like a mountainous collection of garbage heap. Discarded papers were almost floating in the air; letters, magazine covers, and decayed books that had lost their sheen were scattered across a table at the far end of the room. Everything was falling apart; sand all over the floor, dirty kitchen, old refrigerator, small bedrooms with shared bathrooms. It looked like many people were living there already.

"I got a float. We'll just throw it on the floor, and you can sleep there," said Kristin to Molly.

"Thank you!"

"Yeah, sure. Don't worry about it. Get some rest. Tomorrow is another day. And let me tell you. It is always a beautiful day in California."

"Thank you," said Molly, lying down on the floaty to take a nap after putting a towel on it.

So, the next day, Molly headed back down to the beach. She was rested enough and felt better about her bright future in California. She was not scared anymore. Therefore, now she was ready and had decided to go up and down to the restaurants and bars and apply for a job.

Suddenly, she found a place looking for a restaurant bar type of establishment. They were looking for a busser dishwasher. So, she applied for it. The owner/manager came out of his office and told her to complete the paperwork. He then asked her for information about herself or her driver's license since she said she didn't drive.

"Okay, fill out the paperwork, and we'll just pay you under the table," said the manager.

"Thank you so much. I'm just starting to make it here. I come from a long way," she said.

"Yeah. Yeah. Yeah!" He says.

So, Molly filled up the paperwork and handed it to him.

"You can start tonight. Be here at 4. Be ready to clean. We sometimes close late as well," said the manager.

"Thank you, thank you very much," said Molly in gratitude.

Molly returned to the restaurant bar that night and ensured it was pretty busy. Then, she changed into her work clothes and started bussing tables. Some people were giving her tips while she was putting them away. She was just amazed at the money she was getting as she had never experienced such a thing before.

That day at the restaurant, a man sitting at the bar started being nice to her. He probably wanted to be friends with her or was just flirting. The guy looked not more than 19 or 20. Soon, he and Molly exchanged some words where it seemed to be a little bit of flirting.

Molly ignored it completely and did her job. When she went home, she was excited to see all the money she got from bussing at the restaurant on the first day. Her friend Kristin was so excited for her.

"You're going to have to get a bank account or hide that money somewhere here," said Kristin.

"Why do you say that, Kris?" asked Molly.

"Things seem to disappear quite often these days, Molly. And I don't want you to be sad. So why don't you hand all that money to me and I'll take good care of it? As long as I live!" Molly laughed out loud.

So, Molly kept the money by her bedside and slept with it all the time. She went to stores and exchanged small bills for large ones, hiding them at home.

Molly went back to work the next day and saw the same guy from last night. He was a curly, long-haired, blonde surfer dude. They looked at each other from across the bar but didn't say anything at first. In a few seconds, a spur of conscience ran through her brain, telling her that it did not seem right to pass him by ignoring him. "At least I should say Hi," said her inner voice. But unfortunately, all she knew about this guy was his name: Mark.

"Hey, Mark," she waved at him.

"Hey, Molly. How are you doing?"

"I'm okay."

"Well, I came here to visit you."

"Really? Thank you."

"No problem. I'll be at the bar."

"Okay. I'll stop by and talk to you soon."

So, Molly started working. She got busy collecting dishes and cleaning tables. Some people left her tips, while others didn't. That day, she hoped to get a little more money by the night's end. She was really excited.

When she was done with work, she went over to Mark.

"Hey! You are done with everything?" he asked her.

"Ah, Naw! Just a little bit left. You tell me what's up?" she said.

"Hmm, nothing. I was just wondering if you feel like getting a drink with me later. Or something to eat tomorrow?"

"Sure. Depends on what time we get out of here tonight. But we'll talk later," said Molly.

"Right. So, I guess I'll see you around."

Molly waved at him and got back to work. When she was done for the day, she sat down at a spot in the restaurant to relax for a bit. Live music was playing in the background while she watched the band play. She knew that someday she would be doing the same. She hoped that maybe one day she could ask her boss, having enough nerve to play there. However, she kept all those thoughts to herself.

Molly and Mark kept hanging out and became a couple. On the other hand, Kristin doesn't know if she trusts him because he's not from her gang. This turned out to be a conflict between the two friends – Molly and Kristin, and as a result, they stopped seeing each other as much anymore.

Molly kept working while Mark kept coming to the bar.

One day, Molly said to Mark, "Do you think the owner would let me play here?"

"Well, he's a friend of mine. I could ask him for you," said Mark.

Molly became happy as a ray of hope appeared in front of her. So, Mark asked the owner to come over. His name was John.

"So, John, you think Molly could give it a shot at performing here?" asked Mark.

John looked over the situation and said, "Well, I've never heard her play. Can she play guitar well?"

She said, "I think so. I've been practicing a long time."

"Yeah, I've heard her. I love it," said Mark.

"We will work on this. I do have a friend in the industry. Maybe you could stop by to play for him. And maybe he can get you set up with the band. We'll see what we can do," said John.

"Let me set it up. Can you come by my apartment someday? He added

Molly and Mark looked at each other and said, "Great."

Molly got back to work while Mark hung out at the bar. She waited for John to contact her regarding the audition. At the end of the night, when she was getting her tips, John came over and said, "Hey, Molly. Here's my address. Can you come by tomorrow? Say noon-ish, for an audition? My friend wants to meet you. Bring your guitar, too."

"Really? Sure. I'll be there. Thank you," said Molly.

She got so excited, grabbed Mark, and headed out to hang out with friends on the beach.

Chapter 6
Survival

The day finally came when Molly was going to visit John, her Boss, at his house. She had to meet a potential agent for which she got up early in the morning. At 9 o'clock, when she and Kristin were about to leave the house, Kristin said, "Let me buy you a cell phone today."

"Are you serious, Kristin?" exclaimed Molly.

"Yes, why not? I saved up some money to get one for you so you can have your own identification." Kristin said.

"Wow! That's great. Thank you, Kristin!"

Both girls set off for the market to get Molly a Tract phone. Kristin put everything in her name in the cell phone store and bought Molly a new phone. Molly was so happy to have a new phone. She hugged Kristin and said, "Don't worry. I'm gonna pay you the money for that every month. Thank you again, Kristin."

"It's okay," said Kristin.

"But you know what? You're gonna need identification sooner or later. I know we can go down to the county building. We can probably find some records. We can even start digging up some records online. Maybe we can find your birth certificate. How about that, huh?" she added.

"Yeah, that is so great. We'll work on that after I come back from my audition." Molly agreed.

It was almost one o'clock now, and Molly was all dressed up, practicing some of her songs as she started heading over to John's apartment and her boss. Molly got there and knocked on the door. Her boss answered the door and said, "Hey, Molly! Come on in." She went inside and saw the guy. At once, she realized that she might have seen him before in the bar. They did some introductions, and Molly sized up the room. She noticed that on the coffee table, there was a mirror with some residue on it. She was feeling a little nervous in her stomach and was starting to sweat. Meanwhile, John, her Boss, offered her a drink.

"Hey, Molly! You want to drink?" Molly looked at him because she knew he knew that she was 16.

"Nah! It's all right." Answered Molly.

Molly's boss's friend asked, "Hey, so you're gonna play some music for me?" Molly said, "Yep, I can. But can I use your bathroom first?" John looked at his friend and smirked, saying, "Yeah, sure. Go ahead!" Molly said, "Okay, cool." She went around the corner and headed down the hall to the bathroom. She turned the fan and the light on and shut the door behind her. She sneaked back toward the front door quietly, grabbing the keys and the wallet on the buffet by the door. She sneaked quietly, heading out to steal John's or maybe his friend's car keys. She got in the car and took off.

At this point, Molly knew she could not go back to Venice Beach or the apartment because they would be looking for her. So once again, Molly was on the run, scared, and didn't know, what her future would be. She had no idea where she would sleep or what to do. But she knew she had to get on State Road 40 with her guitar and head towards Tennessee. She knew that if she seriously wanted to have a career, then that was where she had got to be.

As Molly ventured further, the strains of country music echoed in her thoughts, a constant companion on her journey. The road stretched ahead like an unwritten story, and she continued to steer her course, fueled by a mixture of determination and uncertainty. Her foot pressed on the gas pedal, propelling her through the night, leaving behind the shadows of her past.

With the weight of the hours pressing upon her, Molly finally sought refuge in the embrace of a truck stop's flickering lights. Nestled within the car's worn interior, she succumbed to weariness, however fleetingly. The symphony of murmured conversations and idling engines became the backdrop to her dreams as sleep momentarily claimed her.

Revived but restless, Molly resumed her expedition, each mile marker a testament to her resilience. The wallet's contents sustained her, a lifeline to another reality she was crafting for herself. The boundaries between states blurred, and memories of her Greyhound bus escape mingled with the aspirations that compelled her forward.

Yet, amid this newfound liberation, Molly's predicament remained a precarious one. The stolen car was an emblem of her audacity, a symbol that alternately thrilled and terrorized her. She navigated the highways with a furtive glance in her rearview mirror, a fugitive caught between freedom and the fear of being caught without a license.

Drawing closer to the threshold of Tennessee, the boundary between her old life and the prospects of a fresh start, an unexpected tableau materialized before her eyes. Flashing lights painted the night sky, a chorus of urgency that jarred her from her reverie. Suspicion clung to her like a second skin, and the question loomed: "Are those sirens for me or the car?"

The California license plate, a badge of her clandestine journey, posed a double-edged question to the world. Fuelled by a cocktail of anxiety and resolve, Molly steered the stolen vehicle into the safety of a truck stop oasis just past Tennessee's border. Emerging from the car's sheltering confines, the chill of the night air bit at her skin. She surveyed her surroundings, each shadow a potential threat, her thoughts swirling in a tempest of apprehension.

Amid this uncertainty, Molly confronted a pivotal choice. The stolen car, an emblem of her recklessness, had to be abandoned. This decision, both heavy and inevitable, settled upon her with a gravity she couldn't ignore. And so, with a final glance, she left behind the car, a silent testament to the sacrifices demanded by her newfound freedom.

Unburdened by the car's stolen weight, Molly embraced the unknown that lay ahead. Her thumb extended like an offering, a beacon of hope in the night's obscurity, as she embarked on a journey of a different kind - hitchhiking, a symbol of trust in the kindness of strangers. The road remained her constant, an uncharted path leading her towards a destiny that was still being written.

Drawing nearer to the heart of Tennessee, each step and ride carved her narrative deeper into the fabric of the land. The road was not just a conduit; it was a companion, a confidant to her secrets, her aspirations, and her doubts. Another truck stop became a temporary haven, a place where fellow travelers' stories intertwined briefly, where connections were forged and left behind in the haze of diesel fumes.

And so, beneath the canopy of stars that bore witness, Molly's journey continued. The stolen car was but a chapter - a thrilling, dangerous prologue to the adventure she was scripting with every footstep and every outstretched thumb. The road stretched ahead, an endless ribbon of possibilities, and Molly walked its path with a heart both heavy and hopeful.

She wanted to go in and use the bathroom. She found a car passing by full of men when she came out. The car slowed down as it neared up around her. One of the guys asked Molly, "Hey! What are you doing here?" Molly didn't talk to them and kept her head down while walking. Finally, she tried to get into the restaurant to use the bathroom.

As soon as she came out of the bathroom, she bumped into a couple trying to converse with her.

"Hey! You alright?" they asked her.

"I'm just a little tired. I don't know those people." Molly replied.

"Come on, let's buy you some breakfast. Come with us. You're safe with us," said the woman.

"You know what, honey? You look like you've been through a lot lately. So, you need some rest and some food," added the man.

Molly went into the truck stop with them; it turned out it was a male and female trucker. They sat down in a booth and started to order breakfast.

Chapter 7
Truckers to the Rescue

Molly entered the restaurant with the male and female truckers, Grey Fox and Red Fox. They were from Tennessee and knew almost everyone in the area, including the waitress. They sat down with Molly, and she didn't feel strange about the couple. She felt safe with them. The couple ordered breakfast for Molly and started talking and consoling her.

After a few minutes, the waitress came over with the breakfast.

"Hey there, Red Fox! How's it going, Grey Fox?" She greeted the trucker couple.

"Hey, Lisa, give Brooke a call for us. Will ya?" asked the lady trucker.

"Sure thing," the waitress replied.

She looked at Molly and said, "Hope you enjoy our grits. They're the best in the county."

"Oh yes, I do like grits so much," Molly smiled back at her normally.

Soon after the waitress left, the three of them got into talking.

"We are around here all the time, and we often see girls like you. All of them are hitchhiking, looking for rides, and end up in truck stations and diners."

"Yeah. But I don't want any trouble, though." Replied Molly

"Don't worry about it. We're not here to get you into trouble. In fact, we're here to get you out of trouble. We're here to help you. We've called up someone, and she's going to be here any minute. Her name's Brooke, and you're going to like her."

Listening to this, Molly started feeling trapped. She wasn't sure what she would do if she was caught up in such a situation. While they kept talking, there came a young girl who was a bit conservative.

"Hey there, you guys," Brooke greeted the trucker couple.

"Can I join you?" she asked them.

"Please do," the couple replied.

"Hi. I'm Brooke," she extended a hand for a shake toward Molly.

"Hey there," answered Molly.

"You must be Molly? Right?"

"Yes, That's me."

"Well, Molly, it's nice to meet you. I'm here to tell you that this couple in front of you helped me in the past. Believe it or not, I was just like you one time before. We have a house with a bunch of bedrooms, a shared kitchen, and a living room. We get kids off the road and give them a place to live until they can get their high school diploma, get into college, or maybe get a job. No one is forced to stay.”

“Really?” Molly asked.

“Yeah, we have some really nice people in this county, and I’m sure you’re gonna like the house.”

“I’m kinda tired right now,” said Molly.

“Trust me. I’ve been to college, and I have devoted my time back. It’s just so great.”

Molly looked at her and somehow felt safe. “That’s cool,” she said.

“I see you have a guitar. We have a music room as well. I’m sure you’ll love it here.”

They sat there for a while and had breakfast. Molly turned to the trucker couple and said, “How can I ever repay you?”

"We just want you to be in a safe place. It is our pleasure. You don't have to feel like you owe us anything."

After they were done eating, the truckers said goodbye to Molly. "Don't worry, Molly. You're in good hands."

As they headed toward the door, a board on the right had pictures of missing children. As they opened the door, a rush of wind came in, pushing up the top layer of the board with pictures in the air. The picture of a missing three-year-old girl suddenly became obvious. This three-year-old girl was Molly, whose picture had been covered since then.

Brooke took Molly to the safe house, which was outside Tennessee.

Chapter 8
Molly Meets the Sheriff

Molly was now in the safe house. She was getting along with everybody and had her own bedroom. She also had some chores around the house that kept her busy all the time. One day, Brooke noticed that Molly had a cell phone. She went up to her and said, "Molly, I think you should turn your cell phone over in case someone is trying to find you. I don't know. Maybe they can track you down, too."

Molly started getting worried about it and went into deep thought. Suddenly, Brooke jolted her out of her contemplation and said, "Why don't we go and meet the Sheriff? He can help us get you a driver's license and identification."

"Sure, yeah, I understand. I don't want any trouble either," said Molly.

"You're not going to be in any trouble. We're all safe here. This is your home. This is where we all came and made our lives," Brooke consoled Molly's troubled mind.

After a few days, Brooke, the counselor, called up the Sheriff's office, where there was another female Sheriff who made the arrangements for Molly to go in and meet the Head Sheriff, Sheriff Don. Molly went in with Brooke.

As she entered the Sheriff's office, she noticed a teddy bear on the back shelf. She kind of looked at it and just touched it. After that, she went on and sat down. The Sheriff looked over at the teddy bear and then looked at Molly. He then just started to ask her questions.

"Molly, I think it's best if we take this cell phone. Is there anybody on here that you don't want us to call or to call," the Sheriff questioned.

"My friend Kristin gave me that phone because I had no identification. And you know, for all I know, she shut it off because she can't afford it. Or she can't find me," replied Molly.

Sheriff Don said, "you know, okay, well, we'll take care of it."

Sheriff started asking her questions again, "How old are you, Molly?"

"16."

"Where are you from?"

"South Dakota."

"Well, why are you here?" inquired the Sheriff.

"Well, I ran away from home because I think I overheard my parents saying that they were going to send me off somewhere and help me go to a place where it would be easier to put me in college without having to pay so much. And in return, my parents' bills would be paid." Molly elaborated on her story.

"Huh? Okay. So then, how did you end up in California?" he asked.

"Well, I ran away, stayed in California, and met some really nice people who helped me get a job. Things were going great until my boss set up an interview and audition because I wanted to be a country star. One of his friends freaked me out. He was a creep. I saw drugs in the room. So, before I got hurt, I stole his car and ran away. I drove and drove and dropped the car off outside Arkansas because of the plates, and then I hitchhiked. That's how I ended up at the trucking station. There, I met Grey Fox and Red Fox, who invited me in, and that's really the whole story."

The Sheriff said, "Okay, okay, great. If you don't mind, I'm just gonna keep the cell phone here. I'm not going to call anybody or interrogate anybody. I just wanna see if anybody tries to call you; I'm not sure they're tracking you. We just want to protect you. You're happy over at the safe house, aren't you?"

Molly said, "Yeah, I'm safe over there, and they are great people. I love the music room."

"Good," said Sheriff Don.

"Well, you and Brooke can now go back to the safe house, and we'll continue our investigation here. No worries. I'll talk to you in a couple of days."

Brooke and Molly got up and left the room. The female Sheriff turned over to Sheriff Don and said, "Wow, she's one of the lucky ones."

"Yeah, sure she is," replied the Sheriff. "Hey, get me the Sheriff of South Dakota on the phone and in Orange County, too."

"Oh, Also, Bud Co Trucking."

"Right away, Sheriff," she said.

Chapter 9

It's Worth A Try

Sheriff Contacts Some Old Friends, The Encounter

The Sheriff, along with the Deputy Sheriff, unite for a search operation. They were on the lookout for the 16-year-old Molly. They searched around the South Dakota area by the Greyhound buses where they suspected Molly to be. They searched through the Greyhound bus stations for some schools not too far away. They went to the schools and started asking questions if there was a girl, about 16 years old, with long brown hair, that went missing. They'd also been investigating and asking people in the Venice Beach area that Molly had mentioned. They asked people at the restaurants and bars, the kids skateboarding and playing volleyball on the beach. They asked them if they had a friend named Molly who had gone missing.

The Sheriff and the Deputy Sheriff were having a bit of really good luck with the search process as they were soon able to track Molly's so-called parents down near the Mexican border. Molly's parents had not yet changed their license plates from South Dakota, which made it easier for the Sheriffs to track them down. So, the Sheriffs contacted the Sheriff in South Dakota for any license plates within the vicinity that were deported. Luckily, the Sheriffs got a positive response, and they were successful in contacting Molly's parents.

In a few hours, the Deputy Sheriff went down along the Mexican border and picked up Molly's so-called parents, bringing them in for questioning. The same happened in the Venice Beach area, where Deputy Sheriff started going into restaurants looking for the girl. At last, they found Molly's friend Mark sitting at the bar. He was very concerned about Molly. However, at the same time, he was also a bit hesitant at first to give the cops any details about Molly. Yet, somehow, the Sheriffs got him talking after a few minutes.

The Sheriff in Orange County also brought in the owner of the bar for questioning. In this way, all of the parties were brought in for questioning.

After a thorough investigation, the Sheriff and Deputy Sheriff found out that they needed to press charges against both of Molly's parents as they were unable to provide the first documents or corroborate their story. The owner of the restaurant where Molly was working had to drop the charges against her because he was paying her under the table. She didn't have any identification or any security number. He had brought the agent in, who he didn't know sold drugs. Deputy Sheriff sent out his team to search this man's house as well in order to prosecute him for providing drugs to a minor.

The Sheriff then decided to contact the Bud Co. Company, a Trucking company outside the Nashville area. He contacted the owners and asked them if they would come in and meet a girl. He was not sure as he was only taking a hunch. He only wanted them to meet her. "Her name is Molly. She's about 16." He told them that they were finding out if she's been raised by a couple who were not her parents.

Chapter 10
Who Am I?

The Sheriff called up the counselor, Brooke, over at the girls' home. And he called in the Deputy Sheriff. Then he said, "Well, ladies, we're trying to find out if there is a possibility that Molly's parents aren't her parents?"

"So, I need your help on how we can dig a little bit without scaring Molly. How to present this? I have an old case that I'm going to bring out. It's about a three-year-old that went missing. And the trucking accident in Tennessee. 13 years ago."

"I don't know if it's Molly. But I'd like to talk to her about her memories. Or how about Brooke talk to her? And then, let's get her in. I want her to take a look at this teddy bear again."

"She walked in one day and kind of glanced at it. I'm going to take it out and put it on my desk. And see if she remembers. I also contacted the owner of Buddy Co., who had a family member that died Christmas Eve, thirteen years ago."

"So, give me some feedback," said Brooke. So, Brooke sat Molly down. She's in the home. She's playing her guitar.

And she said, "Molly, I'd like to talk to you about something that may be a little scary for you."

"It could be just a hunch and may make no difference. But I just want to ask you a few questions."

Molly said, "Sure."

Brooke said, "Please share some of your earliest memories growing up."

Molly said, "Well, I have memories. With my parents."

"I have these memories that I can't explain."

"What do you mean?" said Brooke

Molly was like, "At one time, we were able to celebrate Christmas and birthdays. I wasn't raised that way. We don't celebrate holidays. My parents don't celebrate birthdays."

So, Molly said, "Oh, that couldn't be me."

Brooke said, "Well, we found your parents. You know, who we think are your parents."

Molly gasped, "I don't want to go back."

Brooke said, "We would never send you anywhere, but Molly, we may have evidence."

"They're not your parents. Yeah, we can't really place your birth in any information. We're trying to help you get your birth certificate and driver's license."

Molly said, "Well, what does this mean?"

Brooke said, "Well, there's a chance you were kidnapped.

Molly gasped again, "What do you mean kidnapped?"

"Well, taken as a young child. I'm not trying to scare you. But we cannot get any information on you. And we've done some really good searching."

And Molly said, "Will my parents take me with someone else? Take me and put me with them. Did they buy me?"

Brooke said, "Well, we really don't have the answers to that, but the Sheriff has been investigating and just wanted to ask you a few questions and maybe for you to meet some people. As I said, it's a hunch, but I would never do anything to harm you, just help you."

Molly thought about it and said, "Well, it's a lot to ponder. Maybe I should just sleep on it."

"Absolutely. Whatever you want. But please let me hold you, snuggle up with your sisters in the house.

Sometimes, facing the truth is scary. But sometimes it's a blessing."

So, Molly went to bed that night and dreamt again of being in a vehicle. Country music blaring. Seeing a man's silhouette. A man, singing. Happy Birthday. A Christmas tree. A teddy bear."

So, the next day, Molly contacted Brooke and said, "Okay, if you think that maybe I'm a different person than who I think I am. Then I want to know, who am I? Let's do it."

Brooke said, "I don't want you to get your hopes up. Because this leads to nothing, and we would start all over again, but this is our first lead. And we think it's a pretty good one."

Brooke said, "I have faith in our Sheriff."

"And there is a file. So, let's go over to the station and look at this file and the pictures; we'll just take it from there. Period."

So, Molly and Brooke went over to the Sheriff's station. "Sheriff." They knocked on the Sheriff's door, and the Sheriff said, "Come on in, ladies, come on in."

So, this time, when Molly went in, the teddy bear was on the desk. And she said, "Huh? This is the teddy bear. Again. I just love it." And the Sheriff said, "Well, I've had that teddy bear for a long time." And Molly just looked at him, perplexed. A file was on his desk.

"I have some pictures of the accident inside."

"You don't want to see the disturbing pictures?" Asked Sheriff

So, he just asked her some questions, the same questions that Brooke asked her, "You think I've had that teddy bear like this?" Asked Molly, and the Sheriff said,

"Well, Molly, I'm sure Brooke told you that we have an old file on a little girl that was taken from her family. It was on the night of an accident early morning; her dad was a truck driver. And he was going for a late haul to make some extra money. He brought his little girl with him. However, he got into an accident when the Sheriff, the patrols, the fire, and the rescue got there. There was a teddy bear and a bag for a little girl. The truck driver did not survive."

Molly just looked at him. "Oh, that's terrible. Do you think he was my father? You think I am that girl?"

"Well, it's not that we think it. However, we want to explore the possibility."

"So, I have someone that I would like for you to meet." He kind of looked at Brooke."

"Sure, I'll meet them," said Molly.

So, Molly and Brooke stood up. Molly looked back at the teddy bear and picked it up. And the door is opened.

And when Molly turned around, she saw two men and a woman.

And the woman looks Molly in the eyes. Molly looks her in the eyes. And after a pause, the woman says. "Hello, Christmas."

Molly started to get tears in her eyes. As the water started to emerge in her eyes, she closed her eyes shut, which helped the tears to slide down from the side of her face and onto the ground. Then she dropped the bear in slow motion, and it hit the floor. Molly just looked at her and said, "Mima. Mima?" And the woman looked at Molly and said, "Yes, Molly, your name is Christmas, and I'm your Mima."

Molly ran over to her and hugged her and cried and cried and cried. Her two Uncles, Robert and Gerry, were there, and they hugged her, and everybody started crying. The Sheriff sat down in his chair and looked at Brooke and the female Deputy Sheriff with amazement on his face.

Nobody could stop crying. Nobody could stop staring. The Sheriff looked at the file on his desk. And he took a big stamp. And he stamped it "solved." The families just stood there and cried.

Molly's Mima said, "Christmas, Christmas. You were born on Christmas Eve. Your name is Christmas."

At that moment, they needed some time. And so, the Sheriff, the Deputy Sheriff, and Brooke said, "Come on, let's go into the other room. We have some catching up to do," and the Sheriff said, "Yeah, I've got some paperwork to fill out."

"Some people to arrest." Christmas looked at the Sheriff. He said, "Don't worry, Christmas. No harm will come to you." Grandma Mima said, "No harm's ever going to come to you again."

And the Deputy Sheriff led them all off into a private room. The Sheriff picked up the phone and said get me, the Sheriff of New Mexico. We need to prosecute Molly's so-called parents for kidnapping."

Chapter 11
The Dream

Christmas's mima asked her to stay with her as she missed her a lot. Christmas was more than willing and excited to go to her mima's because she had just found a family. She has just discovered herself with all the answers to her dreams that she has been having all along. She previously thought she didn't belong there, but now she did.

Christmas returned to say goodbye to all her friends at home and gathered all her belongings along with her guitar. She was finally going to her Mima's house. When she got there, the family gave her a warm reminiscing while hearing stories about her parents. It included all her uncles and cousins, who cried and welcomed her to the family. They spent the night looking at some old pictures.

After a while, Christmas started to get a little tired. Her mima said that she had some more exciting news to share with her. However, on the other hand, she also thought that maybe this was all too much for the day. So, she brought Christmas into a spare bedroom in her house. Christmas decorations were everywhere in that room, with a beautiful little Christmas tree in the corner. There were also pictures of her father and mother, pictures of her as a baby. All of Christmas when she was three and younger. She also heard how her mom died during birth, how much her dad loved her, and how close they were. She took those wonderful, heartfelt stories with her as she went to bed and dreamt.

She opened her mind to the things she was blocking out before and had beautiful dreams of flashbacks from her childhood that she could remember. However, there were some sweet memories that, now, Christmas wasn't blocking or thinking they were weird nightmares.

This was how she built a connection with her cousins and Uncles, Rob and Gerry, in the family. She had that evening to herself as she lay in bed dreaming and trying to piece it all together. She finally felt safe and prayed to God. She was extremely thankful.

Christmas was still at her grandmother's place, and she was getting to know her Uncles, Rob and Gerry, and cousins, as well as the town. She was learning about her history and seeing pictures. Today, her grandmother had decided that she had something special she wanted to share. She knew that Christmas that her parents had a home that they had gotten as they had just received the loan, and it was her father's Dream to have a trucking company. But her grandmother wants to take her to the house, and she explains to Christmas, "We kept your father and mother's house. We knew you'd be back. The community was all behind finding you. We never gave up. The church has talked about you all the time, so we didn't sell your parents' house. We saved it for you for when you would come back. Are you ready to go over to see it now?"

Christmas thinks about it and says, "Yes, but do I have to move?" and Christmas's grandmother says, "No. When you're ready and older, it's yours to do with whatever you want. You can sell it, you can remodel it, but it's your home, and it's your parents' home, and we want to give it to you, but of course, you're always welcome here."

So, the next day, there is a big buzz around that Christmas is going to go to her house. She thinks she is just going to go over and see her parents' house. Her house. So, they get in the car. It's near dark now. Just before dark, Christmas and her grandmother get in the car to go over to their parents' home. Christmas is finally home, and they pull into the driveway. It's not an extravagant home. It's a three-bedroom Ranch, but it's been very well-manicured and has trees and rocky edges all around it.

Christmas and her grandmother pulled into the driveway and approached the front door. Christmas's grandmother hugs her and says, "You ready?" And Christmas replies, "Yes." And so, they open the door and notice that nothing has changed. Not even the Christmas tree. They had a real one. It was decorated the same way and was still by the window. Christmas just walks in and sees pictures, the fireplace, and the kitchen and is flooded with memories of family, get-togethers, and people singing happy birthday to her and the tree in the background at the same time. Christmas and her grandmother walk into the nursery or what would have been her bedroom, and it's still all the same with the little bed and her toys. Christmas just goes in there and kind of cries a little bit. She has some memories, but not a lot; she feels sad that she can't remember everything and sits there for a while, touching the toys and looking in the closet. Her little dresses are hung up there. She gets teary-eyed, turns to her grandmother, and says, "Well, I guess I've outgrown this bed." And they kind of laugh.

Then Grandma takes her into her parents' bedroom. And that's when Christmas is a little overwhelmed with memories because she was always afraid to sleep in her bedroom by herself. So, she was always in bed with her father, even the night when her father got the call to take a haul on Christmas Eve.

She was lying there in bed with her father, and she remembered cuddling up with her teddy bear and her father, and that's when she was flooded by a barrage of emotions as she laid down on the bed and curled up in a ball and started to cry. Finally, her grandmother comes over, rubs her hair, and says, "It's okay. They'll always be with you."

They just sit there for a while, and her grandmother holds her. Then, finally, Christmas looks around and says, "Yeah, I know, it's just sad. And I never really was able to have these feelings and share these memories."

They go back through the house and look at the bathrooms and the backyard. "There's room for a pool," Grandma says, "your father and mother always wanted to put a pool in. So, we'll put a pool in if you decide to keep the house. But we want you to go to college, and we want you to stay with us. So, it's all up to you. What do you want to do? The world is your oyster now."

They sit in the kitchen, and Christmas opens the refrigerator and says, "My gosh, these appliances are ancient," while giggling.

Then she opens up the cupboards and says, "I think I'd like to have a pet."

"Absolutely," Grandma says. "We want you to have pets, and whatever you need, whatever you want, you're home now. You're safe. We're your family. In a couple of days, we'd like to take you to the cemetery,"

Christmas's face lights up. "Like, wow, I forgot about that part." Then, Grandma added, "Yes, they are buried at our local cemetery, side-by-side."

Christmas puts her head down and starts getting teary-eyed again. And her grandmother says, "You know, Christmas, while there are many sad things to remember, we want this to be a happy time, too. The family wants you to be happy that you're here."

"All your parents would want was for us to find you. You're safe, you're unharmed, and you're back home. So, we have a little surprise for you…. Well, I told you that the town and the churches and everybody have been looking for you for many, many, many years, and they all decided they would make your Christmas, your first Christmas home, the best Christmas ever."

Christmas's face lights up once again. "What's going on?"

Grandma says, "Well, there are some special people. From what I can hear, they have gathered outside. They're all out there. And your Uncle Rob has put together a special event as well."

They open the door, and there's a little bonfire going on, and people are sitting in chairs all over the front and all up and down the street. Some tables are being set up, and food is being brought. Christmas's eyes are wide open. And she says, "Is this all for me?" And her grandmother says, "Yep. This is our community, and even some special guests are here." One of the biggest beautiful country stars of Tennessee walks up just then. She is well-known. She comes up and says, "Hello, Christmas," and hugs her. "Christmas, we've been looking for you for a long time, and I am here to let you know that there will be a scholarship for you for music, and I am providing it for you. So, I want to encourage you to keep singing and writing songs. And I will do whatever I can to ensure you're encouraged and have opportunities you've never had before."

Christmas just stares at her while crying and responds, "Thank you. Thank you." And she hugs the country star. The country star added, "And I have someone else I want you to meet, too."

Right from behind her back, she walked towards Christmas, a TV show country star, who said in a deep voice, "Hello, Christmas, welcome home. We also want to give you an opportunity to try out for our show to meet producers and to further your aspirations in your dreams to be a country music singer and songwriter."

Christmas just couldn't believe that she was meeting two idols of hers.

Christmas's grandmother says, "Now let the festivities begin. Go join that circle. Sit down with your guitar, and let's sing some Christmas songs." The famous female country star takes Christmas by the hand. And they sit down in the circle and start to play Christmas carols.

Just then, coming down the street, Christmas can see and hear the rumble. It's semi-trucks... semi-truck after semi-truck after semi-truck. And it's not a big street, so you can hear it. The first semi that goes by is Bud Co &

Company, and it's decked out in Christmas lights. On the side of the semi-truck, it says, "Merry Christmas, welcome home, our Christmas."

One semi goes by, and another Bud Co & Company truck goes by, and another Bud Co & Company's decorated semi goes by, and another and another.

Christmas's parents' dream was to own a trucking company, and his brothers had fulfilled that dream and now owned Bud Co. & Company's semi-trailer truck hauling business.

Behind the Bud Co. trucks, the whole town made a Christmas parade, which started to pass right on the street. All night, people come over to enjoy the parade. The whole town shares food, singing, and songs. And the last thing that happened was they never shut the front door.

So, the front door of Christmas's house is open again. And on her Christmas tree are traces of her parents. The night Christmas was born, Christmas Eve, the last thing her mother had done before her water broke was to place an angel on the Christmas tree.

And just like that, a wind came through the front door, just a light breeze, and that angel swayed with the wind.

Christmas remembered what her father had said the night he died. He said, "Don't worry. Mommy angel is looking out after us.

About the Author

Sharon Jank is a woman of many talents and a mother of many talented children. Having grown up in Buffalo, NY, she was a cheerleader for the Buffalo Bills while also working as an x-ray technician at Sisters Hospital. She is passionate about supporting first responders and veterans and donates to homeless shelters, children's homes, and animal shelters. Sharon is also a part of various charity organizations that focus on American heritage, such as the Mayflower Society, Daughters of the American Revolution and Colonial Dames XVII Century.

Sharon's life experiences have shaped her writing style, which is both engaging and heartfelt. Her debut novel is a testament to her passion for storytelling, her love for her hometown, and her late father, who was a trucker in his later years. When she's not writing, Sharon can be found participating in her community in the Tampa Bay area and spending time with her husband and family.

Thank you to all the Truckers, Law Enforcement, First Responders, Counselors, Doctors, and Nurses who put others' lives before their own.

Please remember, if you See something, Say something.

Stop Human Trafficking!